CELEBRATING THE FAMILY NAME OF ZHOU

Celebrating the Family Name of Zhou

Walter the Educator

Silent King Books
a WhichHead Entertainment Imprint

Copyright © 2024 by Walter the Educator

All rights reserved. No part of this book may be reproduced in any manner whatsoever without written permission except in the case of brief quotations embodied in critical articles and reviews.

First Printing, 2024

Disclaimer

This book is a literary work; the story is not about specific persons, locations, situations, and/or circumstances unless mentioned in a historical context. Any resemblance to real persons, locations, situations, and/or circumstances is coincidental. This book is for entertainment and informational purposes only. The author and publisher offer this information without warranties expressed or implied. No matter the grounds, neither the author nor the publisher will be accountable for any losses, injuries, or other damages caused by the reader's use of this book. The use of this book acknowledges an understanding and acceptance of this disclaimer.

Celebrating the Family Name of Zhou is a memory book that belongs to the Celebrating Family Name Book Series by Walter the Educator. Collect them all and more books at WaltertheEducator.com

USE THE EXTRA SPACE TO DOCUMENT YOUR FAMILY MEMORIES THROUGHOUT THE YEARS

ZHOU

Zhou, a name that spans the years,

A story told through joy and tears.

From ancient halls to modern days,

Its light endures, its spirit stays.

With roots in soil both rich and vast,

The Zhou name honors its noble past.

A legacy built on wisdom's stone,

A lineage strong, forever known.

Through rivers wide and mountains tall,

The name of Zhou inspires all.

A steady force, a guiding flame,

A heritage wrapped in endless acclaim.

The Zhou name speaks of boundless grace,

A legacy etched in every place.

From scholars' pens to warriors' might,

It shines as constant as the night.

Through every dawn, in every breeze,

The Zhou name whispers through the trees.

A melody of pride and care,

A history rich, beyond compare.

In bustling streets or fields of green,

The Zhou name's honor can be seen.

A tapestry of strength and love,

A symbol pure, like stars above.

With courage vast and dreams that soar,

The Zhou name opens every door.

A family bound by heart and hand,

Its legacy graces every land.

The phoenix rises, bold and true,

Its wings emblazoned with the Zhou hue.

A name that carries hope and fire,

A story time will not retire.

Through shifting tides and winds that blow,

Unshaken stands the name of Zhou.

Its roots grow deeper, its branches wide,

Forever blooming with steadfast pride.

So here we honor the name of Zhou,

A light that leads where others go.

In every heart, its spirit grows,

A timeless tale the world bestows.

ABOUT THE CREATOR

Walter the Educator is one of the pseudonyms for Walter Anderson. Formally educated in Chemistry, Business, and Education, he is an educator, an author, a diverse entrepreneur, and he is the son of a disabled war veteran.
"Walter the Educator" shares his time between educating and creating. He holds interests and owns several creative projects that entertain, enlighten, enhance, and educate, hoping to inspire and motivate you. Follow, find new works, and stay up to date with Walter the Educator™

at WaltertheEducator.com

www.ingramcontent.com/pod-product-compliance
Lightning Source LLC
LaVergne TN
LVHW052009060526
838201LV00059B/3935